Blessings For Generations Mother Teach Me How to Pray

By: Lorenzo C Spencer

Blessings for Generations Mother Teach Me How to Pray
© Copyright 2016 All rights reserved worldwide. By: Lorenzo C. Spencer

Spencer Truth Publishing

ISBN-13: 978-0692300725

Scripture quotations marked (NKJV) are taken from the New King James Version®. Copyright © 1982 by Thomas Nelson, Inc. Used by permission. All rights reserved.

Scripture quotations marked (NIV) are taken from the Holy Bible, New International Version®, NIV® Copyright © 1973, 1978, 1984, 2011 by Biblica, Inc. Used by permission. All rights reserved worldwide.

Scripture quotations marked (NIV1984) are taken from the Holy Bible, New International Version®, NIV® Copyright © 1973, 1978, 1984 by Biblica, Inc. Used by permission. All rights reserved worldwide.

King James Version (KJV) by Public Domain

All rights reserved. No part of this publication may be reproduced, stored in a retrieval system, transmitted in any form or by means- electronic, mechanical photocopy, recording, or any other- except for brief quotation in print reviews, without the prior permission of the publisher and author.

Printed in the United States of America

Acknowledgements

I would like to thank God for allowing me the opportunity to write this book. I thank him for his Holy Spirit and his inspiration on the pages of this book. I thank him for hearing my prayers and honoring my request to be able to write a book on prayer for children.

I would like to thank my wife. I would like to thank my daughter for inspiring me. I pray blessings over her life. I pray blessings over the lives of all of my nieces, nephews, and little cousins as well. I pray that this book unlock God's blessings that will last for generations. I pray that our family will keep God's word within our hearts for generations. I also pray that God will bless every child throughout the world who read this book. I pray that God's word will last within their families' hearts for many generations.

I would like to thank all of the mothers, fathers, and grandparents who teach their children how to pray.

Contents

Acknowledgements 3
Chapter 1 5
QUESTIONS 5
God Is 6
Who loves you? 7
Who do you talk to? 8
How do you talk to God? 9
What is Praying? 10
Does God listen? 11
What if? 12
Will God answer me? 13
My parents do not give me everything I ask for? ... 14
Why do I have to wait? 15
Chapter 2 21
PRAYING 21
Chapter 3 54
SCRIPTURES 54
Chapter 4 76
Multiply Choices 76
Chapter 5 83
More PRAYERS 83
Chapter 6 Other things 96
Conclusion 104

Chapter 1
QUESTIONS GOD Loves YOU!

God Is

Who is God? God is most powerful than anything or anybody. God is wonderful. God is awesome. God is love. God is helpful. God is caring. God is all knowing because he knows everything. God sees everything. God created us, so he is our Father.

Isaiah 12:2 (KJV)

² Behold, God is my salvation; I will trust, and not be afraid: for the LORD JEHOVAH is my strength and my song; he also is become my salvation.

Who loves you?

   Think about who loves you the most in your life. Is it your mother? Is it your father? Is it your grandparents? Whoever it is God loves you more. God loves you more than everyone in your life that loves you all put together.

Who do you talk to?

Do you talk to your friends every day? Do you talk to your mommy and daddy every day? Do you talk to your brothers and sisters every day? There is someone that you talk to every day. God wants you to talk to him every day. God takes great pleasure in each moment that you take time out to talk with him.

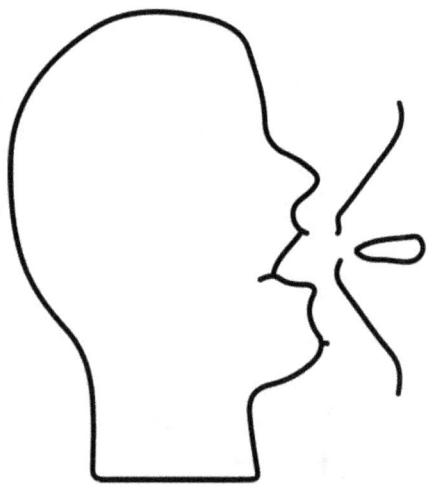

How do you talk to God?

How do you talk to God? You talk to God by praying. Every morning you can say, "Hello God and thank you for loving me. Amen!" At night you can say, "Thank you God for this day. I love you. Amen!"

What is Praying?

Praying is to share your thoughts and feelings with God. If you are hungry, then you would ask your parents for something to eat. If you want your parents to buy you something, then you will tell them what you would like to have. You see, you are sharing your thoughts and feelings with your parents. Praying is to speak and share your thoughts and feelings with God.

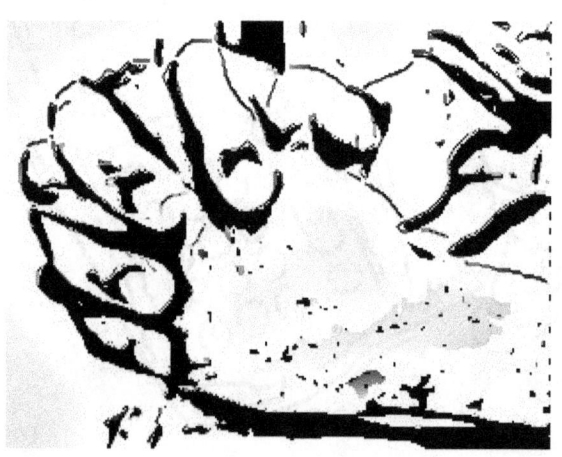

Does God listen?

Does God listen to me? Yes, God listens to you. He listens to your prayers and your thoughts about him. Why? God listens to you because God cares about you. God is a caring father full of love for his child. Oh yes, you are God's child.

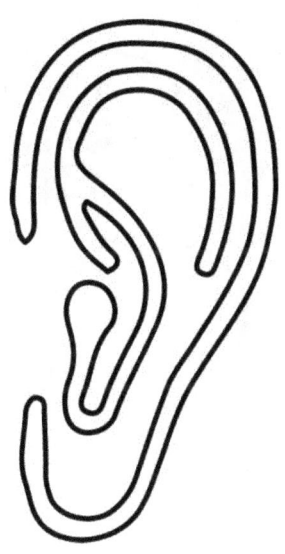

What if?

What if I want to talk to God at lunch? What if I want to talk to God after school? What if I want to talk to God in the middle of the night, because I woke up with a bad dream? Will God listen to me then? You can talk to God at any time. God never sleeps. God will listen to you when no one else will listen to you.

Will God answer me?

Will God answer me? Will God give me what I prayed for? Your parents will give you what you want if you obey them. God is your father. God will always provide us with what we need. God will give you what you pray for when you obey him, and if it does not harm you. How do I obey God? You obey God by following his instructions that he told us to follow in the bible.

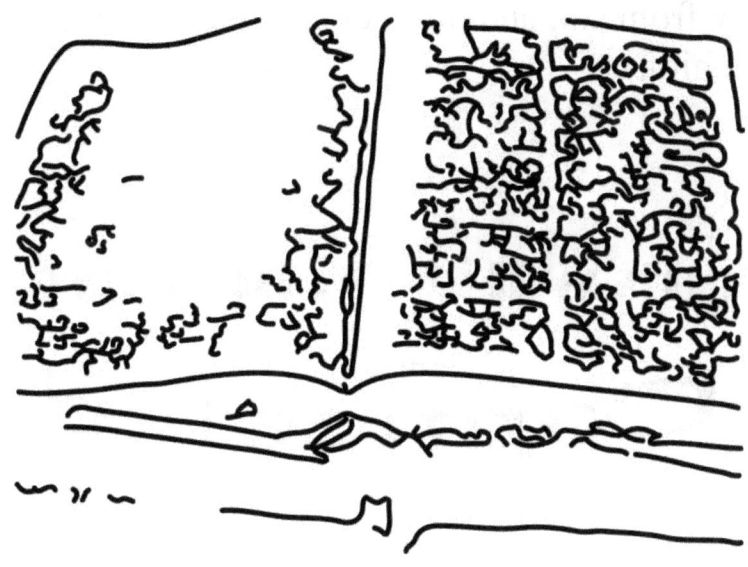

My parents do not give me everything I ask for?

Sometimes, my parents do not always give me what I ask for. Your parents do not always give you what you ask for because it might harm you. A parent's job is to keep the child safe. God will not give you a gift that is harmful. He is a God of love. Your prayers have to be connected with God's will. God's will is for us to be happy, stay away from sin, and have a personal relationship with him.

God's will   Your prayers

[**Connected**]

Why do I have to wait?

I have to wait when I ask my mother for something. Do I have to wait on God to answer me back? Just like when you ask your mother for something, sometimes you will get it right then but at other times you might have to wait. So yes, sometimes you will and sometimes you will not have to wait on God. But, just remember that God will answer your prayers on his time.

You may have to wait or you may not have to wait on God.

Can I trust God?

Can you trust your parents? Who can you trust? If you have good parents, then you should be able to trust them. Can you trust your friends? You should always remember you could completely trust God. God will never let you down. God is trustworthy. You can share with God anything. God will protect your information. You should always pray with faith and confidence. If it is God's will, then you can trust that he will give you what you pray for.

You can trust God!

I do not like to obey

Why do we have to obey God? We are God's children. Smile! Yes, you are God's child. You thought that you only had one father. Guess what, God is your father too. God gives us direction, so we can have a happy life. He does not want to see us hurting ourselves. Your mother will not want you to walk across the street without looking both ways. Why? Because you might get hit! If you obey your mother by doing what she said, then you are prepared to watch out for the cars. By obeying the rules, it will reduce your chances of getting hurt. In a similar way if we obey God, then we can stay under God's shield of protection.

I am God's Child

What if I get tired of waiting?

Sometimes we get tired of waiting because we lack patience. Patience is the opposite of wanting something done quick or fast. It takes patience to wait on your mother to get finished stirring the cake mix, so you can lick the cake bowl. You also got to have patience when you ask God for something.

What is faith?

Faith is you believing in God who you have not seen yet. Faith is you believing in something that has not happened yet. You must first believe before you can expect anything from God. Praying and believing that God can do the impossible is the total sum of faith.

God can do the impossible.

Remember to tell

Just like you remember to tell your mother that you love her; always remember to tell God that you love him. God always remember to tell us that he loves us. God gives us the breath of life each morning to wake us up to see another day.

I Love You God
I Love You God
Thanks for loving me
I love you God
For you have blessed me

Chapter 2
PRAYING

Did You Forget to talk to God today?

All prayers will be in *Italics*.

What if I do not know what to pray for?

If you do not know what to pray for, then say whatever is on your heart. There is no form to praying. There is no correct or wrong way to pray. You should always remember that it is your special time with God. A prayer can be long or it could be very short like *Thank you God, Amen*. God just wants you to mean what you pray for. Some grownups call it heartfelt. It is heartfelt because it is your thoughts and feelings that you are sharing with God. It is your time to ask questions and share things with God.

Ask Questions

If it is your first time taking out the trash or washing dishes, then someone will have to show you how to perform that task. Normally the person who teaches you will tell you, "Please do not hesitate to ask questions if you do not understand." You should not hesitate to ask God a question if you do not understand anything in your life. God will help you understand because he is all knowing. God is full of all wisdom.

Repeat the Question

After your teacher explains the math lesson, you might have a question. So you raise your hand, then you ask her to explain it again. She explains it again, and then you get a better understanding. But, you are still lost. Should you ask again to get a better understanding or should you pretend that you know how to do it? You should ask again, so you can get a better understanding. Likewise if you already have asked God a question several times and you still do not understand, then you should continue to ask God so that the answer will be clearer. You should never be afraid to ask God a question over, if you are clueless of his answer the first time or first couple of times.

Listen to God

Most parents want you to be open with them. They want you to share your accomplishments, achievements, and disappointments. God wants you to do the same with him. God wants you to be open to talk with him about anything.

When you share your problems or talk in general about how your day went with your parents, sometimes your parents will give you advice. If you do not listen, it will not help you. As God guide you through your life, you must be able to listen to God. God will provide you with instructions that could keep you safe if you listen. It is up to you to take God's advice. Whether you obey or disobey God's voice that is your choice.

God always welcome you to talk with him

Your earthly parents might tell you, from time to time, that you can always come and talk to them when you need too. God always welcome you to come and talk to him at any time as well. God invites you to tell him what is on your mind. God already knows what is on your mind, but God wants you to be comfortable enough to ask him anything and tell him anything. Once you are comfortable, your relationship will begin to grow deeper with God. Always remember if you cannot depend on anyone else, you can always count on God.

How did Jesus teach his disciples how to Pray?

Matthew 6:9-15(NKJV)

9 In this manner, therefore, pray:
Our Father in heaven, Hallowed be Your name.
10 Your kingdom come.
Your will be done
On earth as it is in heaven.
11 Give us this day our daily bread.
12 And forgive us our debts, As we forgive our debtors.
13 And do not lead us into temptation,
But deliver us from the evil one.
For Yours is the kingdom and the power and the glory forever.
Amen.

What did Jesus tell his disciples about Prayer?

Jesus told his disciples to ask for what they wanted in his name. We follow the instructions that Jesus gave his disciples, so we end our prayers in Jesus's name also. Why? There is power in Jesus's name. God gave Jesus a name that is above all other names.

John 14:13-14(KJV)

13 Whatever you ask in my name, this I will do, that the Father may be glorified in the Son. **14** If you ask me anything in my name, I will do it.

Praying for Strength

Grownups are not always strong. Sometimes they need strength too. They get their strength by calling on Jesus. Jesus will give you strength if you need it. When you are feeling weak, then you can call on Jesus for strength too. Jesus is our source of strength in times when we feel like we cannot make it.

Jesus, give me strength

Jesus, I need strength

I believe that you will give me strength

Thank you Jesus

Because I can do all things through you

You are the source of my strength

Praying to like Self

You should learn how to like yourself. Do you look in the mirror because kids call you names? Do you think that you are not perfect? You are a beautiful (girl) or a handsome (boy) because God made you. He made you different but special. God made you perfect in his own way, so smile and start liking yourself.

God thank you for making me

Help me gain self-confidence

Help me with my self-esteem

Thank you for loving me

Sometimes my peers can be so mean

Help me love you

Help me love them

Help me love myself

Praying for help in School

Are you having a hard time in school? You are not alone because many kids have a hard time in school. Do you study hard, but you cannot seem to get it? Why not pray about it? God cares enough about you that he will even help you with your schoolwork. God can increase your knowledge or send someone to tutor you in the subject that is troubling you.

God help me with my schoolwork

God help me understand

God help me grow stronger in this subject

That I may be able to comprehend

Praying for Love

Do you feel like no one loves you? Are your parents never around? Are they around but do not listen to you? Are you thinking about hanging with the wrong crowd to get some love? If they are the wrong crowd, then they will never love you any way. They will only lookout for themselves. If you feel this way, it is a perfect time to talk with God.

God I do not feel love
God touch my heart
With your love
Touch my parents' hearts
That they may listen to me
Bless my parents with a good job
So they can be around to raise me up
Surround me with friends
Who truly loves you and me too!

Praying to feel in place

Do you feel like the odd ball because you are doing the right things? When it seems that everyone else around you is doing the wrong things, never forget, Jesus was odd too. Jesus stood up for the right things. How can you get over those feelings? Only God can help you get over those feelings. You have to **pray about it.**

God give me joy and peace

That I do not feel like an odd ball anymore

Let me be happy

With much joy

For standing up for the right things

Make my heart merry

Help me get over my uncomfortable feelings

While I continue to do the right things

Praying that I will not be afraid

What if I am afraid to go to sleep because I have bad dreams? What if I am afraid of the bully that is picking on me? You do not have to be afraid. All you have to do is ask for God's help, so you will not be afraid anymore. God will replace that fear with his love. God's love will give you strength. This strength comes from knowing that God is always protecting you.

God take away my fear

Replace it with your love

That I will not be afraid anymore

Filled me with your joy

Let me have good dreams

Give me the courage, so I won't be afraid of the bully anymore

Praying about a Bully

I feel like my classmates are always bullying me. They keep talking about my clothes and shoes. They even talk about my hair. God my parents are doing the best that they can. Why do the kids dislike me? Other kids are mean because sometimes they do not know any better. You should always remember that you are somebody because you are God's child.

God my parents are trying to provide a good home for me

I thank you for them

God, make the bullies stop messing with me

I love you God

I am somebody

Because you love me

Even though, they treat me like nothing

God continue to bless them and me

How a Bully Feels

Lord, I feel like I have to make people like me. Some people call me a bully. I feel like I have to protect myself because I don't have what they have. The other children don't understand my struggles. I have a lot going on in my life, and it seems like no one even cares. I am seeking you God for answers.

God, help me

If I am a bully

Lord, help me change

Give me peace

Give me self-confidence

So I don't have to worry about what people think

God pour your love upon me

God heal me of fear, sadness, and loneliness

Lord, help me stop being a bully

Praying about Peer Pressure

God, should I give in to pure pressure? My friends want me to do something that I know it is against your will. God, how can I say no without looking silly? One thing that you should know is most grownups have been in a similar situation. You have to stay strong.

God give me the strength to say no

God give me the strength to walk away

God make a way that I can get out

God tell me what to say

God help me escape pure pressure

God encourage me

God keep me

Praying for my Parents

God my parents are catching it rough with bills and other things. What can I do to help them out? They keep arguing all the time. God, there is no peace in our house. Plus, my parents seem like they do not understand me.

God, it is me

Your child

Let peace be in our house

Bless my parents

So, they can do better

Help me be a better child

Bless our whole family

I pray that my parents understand me

Praying on how to forgive

God just the other day a person made me mad. I got very angry. I feel an unpleasant feeling every time that I am around this person now. God, I know that is not right. God how can I forgive that person?

God help me forgive this person

You have forgiven me

Help me get over this hate

Replace it with mercy and grace

Let me forgive from my heart

Replace any sign of envy

With love from you God

Guard my thoughts against unforgiveness

Protect my heart against unforgiveness

Always Give Thanks

God does not have to bless you, but God bless you every day. Your mother does not have to buy you anything that you want. Your mother buys you gifts because she loves you. God gives us good things because he loves us more than our parents. We should always give thanks for the good things that God gives us. We should give thanks to our parents as well.

Thank you Lord

Thank you Lord for my blessings

Thank you Lord

Thank you Lord for everything

Thank you Lord for your kindness

Thank you Lord for your goodness

Remember God can fix it

God can solve all your problems if it is his will. God knows your problems, but you still have to ask him for help. Just like the teacher knows, the answers to the math problem that she gave you. If you do not understand how to get the answer to the question, then you will have to ask her for help. God wants you to learn how to trust in him. You build up trust in God when you ask God things that you do not understand, and you rely on him to help you.

I need your help God

Please fix my problem

I cannot fix it myself

God, please help me

There is more to live for

Did you have a bad day today? If yes, everyone has a bad day. Sometimes it seems like you are having a bad month or week. You should always remember that things will get better. When you feel like there is nothing to live for, there is everything to live for. Troubles do not last always.

God give me a peace of mind

It seems like nothing is going right

Let me feel your joy and peace

So that I know everything is alright

Take away these bad thoughts

That I am feeling toward life

Uplift my heart

Give me the strength to push forward in life

Praying for Wisdom

Do you know what wisdom is? Some grownups do not know what wisdom is. If not, you are not by yourself. If you already know what wisdom is then you have an advantage over everyone else. Why not pray for more wisdom or ask God the giver of wisdom to give you wisdom.

Lord, give me wisdom

I ask for wisdom

I pray for wisdom

Place in my heart wisdom

Because you know all things

There is nothing

That you do not know

Lord, I seek wisdom

Place wisdom in my heart

Praying for Truth

One of the most important things is to know the truth. A lie will only complicate the situation. Bob knew that his go-kart ran on gas. He told his little sister that his go-kart ran on water. She filled it up with water one day. When Bob went to turn it on, it would not start. If Bob would have told the truth to his sister, then he will still be able to ride his go-kart. The water that Bob's sister put in his go-kart messed up his engine. If you know the truth, then you can make better judgment calls or decisions. That is why it is very important to ask God for understanding of his truth.

Father as I grow older

Let me grow in the truth

Let me never forget the truth

Bless me to know the truth

Even in my youth

Praying for Understanding

Have you ever wanted to do something but you never understood how to do it? If you do not understand the directions, then the directions are useless. They become just words or pictures. The directions are only great instructions when you understand them. We must pray for understanding.

God I ask for understanding

I pray to know more about you

I pray for more understanding on how to please you

I ask for understanding

Understanding of my parents

Understanding of myself

Understanding of my schoolwork

God, I pray for more understanding

Because I can understand nothing by myself

Praying to better understand how to love God

You might feel like you do not know how to love God. It may seem easier to love your mother and father than God. It is awesome loving God because God is wonderful. God loves us even when we do not understand how to love him.

If you are feeling that way, then ask God to show you how to better love him.

God help me to better understand how to love you

You love me

I pray to know

How to love you more

Help me understand how to love you more

Because your love brings peace, happiness, and joy

Praying for Knowledge

If you ever want to understand knowledge, then ask God to give you knowledge. God can provide you with knowledge that is not taught in college. You should always remember that going to college is a good thing but to ask God for knowledge is a better thing. Why? God created the universe, so he knows everything about all things.

God give me knowledge

Place knowledge in my heart

Let your knowledge never depart

From me

So that wisdom

I will keep

So that I will always remember to seek

You God

I want to be a person after your own heart God

Praying for Joy & Peace

If there is ever a moment when you are feeling frustrated, then you can ask God to give you his joy and peace. God will give us his peace and joy. God's peace is beyond understanding and his joy is a sure delight.

I ask for joy

I ask for peace

God keep watching over me

Fill me this moment

With your joy

With your peace

Renew me

Lord, uplift me

So that I will be happy

So that I might feel the presence of your peace

Praying to Understand Your Purpose

You have a purpose. What is a purpose? A purpose is something that you were called to do by God. Oh yes, God has something for you to do. You are special. Everything in life has a purpose just like the purpose of food is to give your body nutrients. God made you for a specific reason. God gave you a purpose.

Lord what is my purpose?

Lord, help me grow into my purpose

Lord reveal my purpose to me in due time

Lord guide me that I will fulfill my purpose in due time

A Prayer for Your Future

God is the only one who knows the future. The future is what has not happen yet. Will you please take a minute and think about how you see your life in the future? I am quite sure that you came up with some interesting things. You should remember to keep God first, and then your future will surely be great.

Lord, I place my future in your hands

My future depend on you

My life is in your hands

Only with you do I really stand a chance

Lord, help me to advance, so that my future will surely be great

Watch what you look at and listen to

If good parents hear a cartoon show cussing or talking about bad things, then they will say, "What is it that you are watching." Immediately they will say, "Change the channel." God wants his children to watch what they listen to and watch what they look at. That includes what games you play and what you look at on the internet. Why? What you watch and listen to could have an effect on your thinking. God wants you to enjoy life, but he wants to protect you from bad things.

Father, help me

You know the things that are bad for me

Father, guard my mind

Father, guard my thoughts

Father, guard my eyes

Father, guard my ears

So that what I look at will not poison my mind

Father, help make the right judgment call

Through Jesus Christ

So that I can be able to

Enjoy all things

But not the things that are offensive to you

Nuggets of Life

1. God is love
2. Never forget to talk to God
3. God loves you
4. You might make a mistake
5. But, God will forgive you
6. Try not to repeat your mistake
7. Keep on trusting in God
8. Keep on praying to God
9. Keep on studying God's word
10. Keep on obeying God
11. Keep on listening to God
12. And God will lead you

Chapter 3

SCRIPTURES

Things to Remember

Obey

Exodus 20:12 (NKJV)

¹² "Honor your father and your mother, that your days may be long upon the land which the LORD your God is giving you.

Sometimes you might feel like you do not always want to listen to your parents. You must show respect towards your parents because that is what God want you to do.

Ephesians 6:1 (NIV)

6 Children, obey your parents in the Lord, for this is right.

Why do parents teach their children about God?

Why do parents teach their children about God? God tells parents to train up a child in the way that they shall go so that their child will know about him. Parents teach their children about God, so that their children may know how to build a good relationship with him.

Proverbs 22:6 (NIV)

⁶ Start children off on the way they should go,
and even when they are old they will not turn from it.

A Borrower

You must learn how to save your money and live within your means. If you borrow just to buy something that you could wait to get, then it will make you a borrower for no reason at all. A borrower is always in debit to the lender.

An Example

You want a video game that cost $6. You ask your mother to buy it for you. Your mother will charge you $2 extra to buy it for you, and $0.50 extra a month until you pay it off. You only get $2 a month for allowance. If you wait 3 months, then you can buy it on your own.

If you choose to let your mother buy it for you now, then you will be out of more money. It will take you 4 months to pay off the original cost of $8. Plus an extra $3 in interests for the 6 months that it will take you to pay her off. You would have paid the total of $11 eventually.

Proverbs 22:7 (NIV)

[7] The rich rule over the poor,
    and the borrower is slave to the lender.

"Sometimes, you have to wait to get a better deal."

Gaining Riches

You can get rich by other means such as doing dishonest stuff. But when you do dishonest things, sooner or later, there will be a price to pay. Most of the time that price will make you sorrowful. I will use robbing people for an example. If you rob people for riches, then you may become rich. But when you get caught, there will be sorrow. Most of the times, you will end up having to serve time in prison, someone might hurt you badly, or you might lose your life. On the opposite side, if you gain riches with the blessings from the Lord, then you will not have to worry about the natural sorrows from trying to build your own riches by yourself.

Proverbs 10:22 (KJV)

The blessing of the LORD, it maketh rich, and he addeth no sorrow with it.

Peace

I know that sometimes that you may feel bad when people do you bad for no reason at all. It is upsetting if you are only trying to be a friend. But, sometimes people will dislike you for no reason at all. How can you find peace when it feels like every day is a battle or a war? God's words say, "He can make your enemy at peace with you." What does that mean? It means they will stop messing with you.

Proverbs 16:7 (KJV)

[7] When a man's ways please the LORD, he maketh even his enemies to be at peace with him.

Proverbs 3:1-2 (NKJV)

3 My son, do not forget my law,
But let your heart keep my commands;
[2] For length of days and long life
And peace they will add to you.

Laziness Leaves You Broke

You can sit on the front porch or play video games all day long, but you will not make any money unless it is your job. It is hard to escape poverty if you are unwilling to work yourself out of poverty. If you work hard and put the Lord first, then there is a profit to be made. You can expect a paycheck at the end of every week or every two weeks. You cannot expect a paycheck if you just sit around the house and talk on the phone without a job once you become a young adult.

Proverbs 14:23 (KJV)

23 In all labor there is profit,
But idle chatter[a] *leads* only to poverty.

Dishonest Money Leaves

When you look at drug dealers, robbers, and people doing things dishonest, they seem to be the one prospering. They have the cars, houses, and money, but it only last a minute. God's word says, "If you work hard for those things (house, car, etc…), then it will last." So there is nothing wrong with working hard to get the things that you want because if you obey God, then it will last.

Proverbs 13:11 (KJV)

[11] Wealth gotten by vanity shall be diminished: but he that gathereth by labour shall increase.

RULES

It might seem that rules are boring and dumb. Why do I have to follow the rules? My parents have rules for me to follow. My school has rules for me to follow. God has rules for me to follow. Rules should be designed to keep you safe from danger. God's word is designed to keep you safe. Also if you continue follow God's word, then God will surely continue to bless you and keep you out of harm's way.

Proverbs 3:3-4 (NKJV)

[3] Let not mercy and truth forsake you;
Bind them around your neck,
Write them on the tablet of your heart,
[4] *And* so find favor and high esteem
In the sight of God and man.

Trust in God with all your Heart

You cannot go to the store with half of a dollar bill and expect to spend it. You have to have the whole one dollar bill connected together in order to buy something. You cannot trust in God a little bit but put more trust within yourself. You must trust in God with your whole heart and let God lead you.

Proverbs 3:5-7 (NKJV)

[5] Trust in the LORD with all your heart,
And lean not on your own understanding;
[6] In all your ways acknowledge Him,
And He shall direct your paths. [7] Do not be wise in your own eyes;
Fear the LORD and depart from evil

I can do all things

You might be afraid to take on a new task because you are afraid to fail. It might seem certain that you cannot do it. You should always remember to pray and ask God for his help. You should say to yourself, "It is possible to do anything with Christ Jesus's help."As long as everything is possible through Christ Jesus, then nothing is impossible.

Philippians 4:13 (NKJV)

[13] I can do all things through Christ who strengthens me

God loves everybody

Does God love everyone else? God loves all of his creation. God dislike sin because sin separates us from God. God is holy. God loves us so much that he made a way for us to overcome sin. We overcome sin through Jesus Christ.

John 3:16 (NIV)

[16] For God so loved the world that he gave his one and only Son, that whoever believes in him shall not perish but have eternal life.

God Cares

If you leave home to go over your cousin's house or grandparent's house, your parents might say, "Do not forget to call home and check in every so often." Why? Your parents just love to hear your voice and mentally want to confirm that you are okay. They are concerned about your well-being. God automatically looks out for your well-being because he is much more concerned about your well-being than your parents are. God loves it when you check in and talk with him daily. God loves you so much that he has a plan for you.

Jeremiah 29:11 (NKJV)

[11] For I know the thoughts that I think toward you, says the LORD, thoughts of peace and not of evil, to give you a future and a hope.

Romans 8:28 (NKJV)

[28] And we know that all things work together for good to those who love God, to those who are the called according to *His* purpose.

God has my future in his hands

You can wait

God wants his children to wait on him and not rush. When you rush things, it will lead to worry. If you pray for something in God's will, then God will deliver it in his timing. God's timing could be now, today, tomorrow, or years from now etc….. One thing for sure and you can have confidence in, if God approves your prayer request, then it shall come to pass.

Philippians 4:6 (NIV)

[6] Do not be anxious about anything, but in every situation, by prayer and petition, with thanksgiving, present your requests to God.

Worrying

A child shouldn't have to worry about anything, let alone schoolwork and household duties. Some children worry about different stuff every day. They worry about will their parents get a divorce. Some children worry about how their parents will pay the rent, utilities, phone bill, and even where their next meal will come from. They worry about if other children will like them or not. You do not have to worry. God's word says, "Do not worry about things that you have no control over." You do not have any control of how tall you will grow, so STOP WORRYING. If anything is bothering you, then talk to God about it.

A Prayer for Worrying

Lord, sometimes I worry

I sometimes worry about what we are going to eat

I sometimes worry about where we are going to sleep

I sometimes worry about doing a great job

I sometimes worry about my parents

Will they get another job?

Lord stop my worrying

I do not want to think about those things anymore

Lord, make provisions for those things and more

Replace my worrying heart

With a heart that is worry free

A heart that trust in you God

What Do You Hope for?

Do you hope to be a doctor when you grow up? Do you hope to be a teacher when you grow up? Do you hope to be a lawyer when you grow up? What do you hope to be when you grow up? Do you hope to be a mature Christian when you grow up? Do you hope to be a man or woman loved greatly by God when you grow up?

Isaiah 40:31 (NIV)

[31] but those who hope in the LORD
   will renew their strength.
They will soar on wings like eagles;
   they will run and not grow weary,
   they will walk and not be faint.

Self-control

From time to time, you might hear your parent say, "Practice self-control." What is self-control? Self-control is to be able to control your emotions and actions under all circumstances, good or bad. If you cannot control yourself, then you will make bad choices. If you know how to control yourself, then you will do what is right most of the time. God wants you to learn self-control and not to get upset quickly.

Galatians 5:23 (NIV)

[23] gentleness and self-control. Against such things there is no law.

A Good Name

Money goes and come, but a good name is hard to repair. People will always remember your name and some names have no credibility. So do not try to get rich by destroying your name. Make sure your profession is honorable. Some people will always view you as a good person or a bad person. So make sure that your name spells out that you are a good person.

Proverbs 22:1(NIV)

22 A good name is more desirable than great riches;

to be esteemed is better than silver or gold.

Seek first his Kingdom and his Righteousness

Most people seek everything else first before they seek God. You can save yourself some troubles and time by seeking God's kingdom and God's righteousness first. God will add everything else. If you seek everything else first, most of the time, you will lose it. You might even have to start over from the bottom and climb your way back to the top.

Matthew 6:33 (NIV)

[33] But seek first his kingdom and his righteousness, and all these things will be given to you as well.

Chapter 4

Multiply Choices

Can you trust in God?

   A) Yes
   B) No

Hint is on page: 16

Does God love you?

   A) False
   B) True

Hint is on page: 7

Who loves you the most?

- A) Grandparents
- B) Mother
- C) Father
- D) God

Hint is on page: 7

How often can you talk to God?

- A) Once a week
- B) Everyday
- C) Anytime you feel like it
- D) Once a month

Hint is on page: 8

How do you talk to God?

- A) Pray
- B) Inbox him
- C) Call him on the cellular phone

Hint is on page: 9

Will God give me peace?

   C) Yes
   D) No

Hint is on page: 48

Can I ask God for wisdom?

   A) Yes
   B) No

Hint is on page: 43

Can I ask God for knowledge?

   A) Yes
   B) No

Hint is on page: 47

Can I ask God for understanding?

    A) Yes
    B) No

Hint is on page: 45

Does God listen to me?

    A) True
    B) False

Hint is on page: 11

Should I worry?

    A) Yes
    B) No

Hint is on page: 70

What is praying?

A) Talking to your mom
B) Talking to God
C) Talking to grandmother

Hint is on page: 10

Will God help me?

A) No, God want help me
B) Yes, God will help me

Hint is on page: 23

Can I always depend on God?

A) Yes
B) No

Hint is on page: 26

Will God look out for me?

   A) Yes
   B) No

Hint is on page: 67-68

What is the name of the Son of God?

   A) John
   B) James
   C) Jesus

Study: John 3:16 / Luke 1:26-39

Did Jesus die?

   A) Yes
   B) No

Study: Mathew 26-28

Did Jesus rise up from the dead?

A) Yes
B) No

Study: **Mathew 26-28**

Chapter 5

More PRAYERS

Learning New Prayers

A Prayer for Success

I want to be successful

But I do not want to leave you God

I want to be successful

Let your word never depart from my heart

My success depends on you

I cannot be successful without you

Lord, show me how to be successful

Lord, bless me that I may become successful

A Prayer for God's Guidance

Lord guide my parents
Lead them in your ways
So they can guide me
Lord guide my teachers
Lead them in your ways
So they can guide me
Lord guide my family members
Lead them in your ways
So they can guide me
Lord personally guide me
Teach me your ways
So I can understand the truth myself
Lord I need your guidance
I look to you for help

A Prayer for Removal of Fear

Lord, take away my fear

Remove it far from me

Replace it with confidence in you

Because you are always near me

Replace it with your love

Because you love me

Take away all of my fears

So that fear is no longer a part of me

A Prayer for God's Protection

Lord watch over my family

Lord watch over me

Lord protect my family

Lord protect me

Put a shield over my family

Put a shield over me

Protect my family against any enemy

Protect me against any enemy

Lord continue to bless my family

Lord continue to bless me

Asking the Lord

Lord, what do you expect of me?

What do you want me to do?

What are your plans for my life?

How can I improve my behavior?

How can I please you?

An Earlier Morning Prayer

Lord thank you for waking me up

Lord thank you for the breath of life

Lord thank you for another morning

In your arms, everything is all right

Guide me through another day

Help me understand my schoolwork

Let me have an awesome day

Cover me with your protection all day

A Bedtime Prayer

Lord, I am blessed

Watch over me

As I rest

Watch over my family

Jesus, stay by my side

Forgive me of my sins

Continue to bless me

Good night God

And continue to bless my family

A Mealtime Prayer

As I eat this meal

Father thank you for the food

That I am about to eat

Bless this food

That it might be

Good for my body

And great to eat

May it provide strength in me

I thank you Lord

For this meal that is in front of me

A Prayer of Thanks

I am happy to be in your presence

I am happy to be your child

I am happy for your love

I bless you with my smile

Thank you God for your mercy

You are with me all the time

Because you are an awesome God

I just want to say thank you

From the bottom of my heart

A Prayer for Sadness

Lord, I feel upset

I feel sad

Uplift me

So that I can feel glad

Dry my tears

So that I can be happy

Give me peace, Lord

I know that you love me

I want to feel happy

Create a Prayer with Your Parents

Create Your Own Prayer

Chapter 6
Other things

God I believe

in you

What is sin?

Sin is anything that is the opposite of God. Sin is anything that is opposite of love. Sin is walking after one's own will and not God's will.

What is Holiness?

Holiness means to be holy. Holiness is a form of righteousness and justice. True holiness can only be accomplished through Jesus Christ.

What is righteousness?

Righteousness means to be right with God. It means to be right in God's eyesight. We can only accomplish this type of righteousness through Jesus Christ.

OT Books of the Bible

Genesis	Psalms	Haggai
Exodus	Proverbs	Zechariah
Leviticus	Ecclesiastes	Malachi
Numbers	Song of Solomon	
Deuteronomy	Isaiah	
Joshua	Jeremiah	
Judges	Lamentations	
Ruth	Ezekiel	
1 Samuel	Daniel	
2 Samuel	Hosea	
1 Kings	Joel	
2 Kings	Amos	
1 Chronicles	Obadiah	
2 Chronicles	Jonah	
Ezra	Micah	
Nehemiah	Nahum	
Esther	Habakkuk	
Job	Zephaniah	

NT Books of the Bible

Matthew
Mark
Luke
John
Acts (of the Apostles)
Romans
1 Corinthians
2 Corinthians
Galatians
Ephesians
Philippians
Colossians
1 Thessalonians
2 Thessalonians
1 Timothy
2 Timothy
Titus
Philemon
Hebrews
James
1 Peter
2 Peter
1 John
2 John
3 John
Jude
Revelation

Do not forget
To pray
And read
your Bible

What do I have to do to be Saved?

You can pray about it and read the below scriptures on being saved. You can also talk with your parents, grandparents, Sunday school teacher, or minister more about being saved so that you may truly understand.

A Prayer

Jesus, lead me in the right direction

Guide my heart in truth

I want to live with you for eternity

Guide me so that I know what to do

What must I do to be saved?

Enlighten my understanding of the true meaning of being saved

Scriptures

Romans 10:9-10

1Cor 15:1-14

Acts 16:30-33

Mark 16:16

John 1:12-17

John 14:1-2

Mathew 26-28

Philippians 4:6-7 (KJV)

6 Be careful for nothing; but in every thing by prayer and supplication with thanksgiving let your requests be made known unto God.

7 And the peace of God, which passeth all understanding, shall keep your hearts and minds through Christ Jesus

Jesus Loves YOU!

Conclusion

God loves you no matter what, so always take time out to talk with God. There are no problems to big that God cannot solve them when you ask him about it in prayer. So if you want to discover more about God, then read your bible and pray daily. You do not have to have a special reason to talk with God. God loved you before you were born. God still loves you now because you are his child. God created you. God wants to have a good relationship with you. As you grow older in life, always remember the secrets in living this life are to trust in God, have faith in God, love God, and obey God. Always remember to keep Jesus first in your life, and God will always bless you throughout your life.

www.ingramcontent.com/pod-product-compliance
Lightning Source LLC
Chambersburg PA
CBHW070303100426
42743CB00011B/2324